Cillian Murphy

A biography

Red BOUTA

© 2024 ALIAREDA

© 2024 ALIAREDA

All worldwide rights of reproduction, adaptation and translation, in whole or in part, are reserved. The author is the sole copyright holder and responsible for the content of this book.

Introduction

This biographical book tells the incredible story of Cillian Murphy, an Irish actor who captivated the world with his dazzling performances. From his promising debut to his memorable role in ' Peaky Blinders ", to his Oscar triumph for the film "Oppenheimer", Cillian has proven himself to be one of the most versatile and acclaimed actors of our time.

In the kaleidoscope of the film industry, Cillian Murphy stands out as a remarkable actor, whose versatile talent and searing intensity have captivated audiences around the world. Originally from Cork, Ireland, Murphy has established himself as one of the most sought-after performers of his generation, leaving an indelible mark on film and television.

The phenomenal Cillian Murphy: A hypnotic gaze and captivating talent

Cillian Murphy, the charismatic Irish actor, has captivated audiences around the world with his hypnotic icy gaze, his irresistible composure and his mysterious and captivating acting. Since his big screen debut, he has risen through the ranks to become a leading actor, known for his unforgettable performances in acclaimed productions.

A title role in Nolan's masterpiece

The summer of 2023, the release of the epic film "Oppenheimer" by the great Christopher Nolan marked a turning point in Murphy's career. In this film, he plays the eponymous scientist, a complex and fascinating character who propelled him to international stardom. His exceptional performance earned him an Academy Award nomination and critical acclaim.

Consecration to the O scars and ambassador of Versace

2023 was a milestone year for Murphy, who won the coveted Best Actor Oscar for his role in "Oppenheimer." This recognition cemented his status as a Hollywood icon and propelled him to new heights.

Alongside his big screen triumphs, Murphy has become the new face of "Versace Icons ", the luxury watch collection from fashion house Versace. Its elegance and refined style perfectly embody the spirit of the brand, underlining its benchmark status in the world of fashion and entertainment.

The Murphy phenomenon

Cillian Murphy phenomenon is built on his unique ability to portray complex, evocative characters with exceptional depth and nuance. His hypnotic icy gaze, irresistible composure and mysterious acting create an unforgettable screen presence that leaves a lasting impact on audiences.

At just 47 years old, Murphy has already achieved a remarkable career and shows no signs of slowing down. His undeniable talent and irresistible charisma will undoubtedly continue to captivate audiences for many years to come.

From his breakthrough role in the post-apocalyptic horror film "28 Days Later" to his haunting portrayal of ruthless gangster Tommy Shelby in the hit series " Peaky Blinders ", Murphy has demonstrated extraordinary depth and range in his choice of roles. His magnetic intensity, charismatic presence and ability to portray complex and tormented characters have made him a favorite of filmmakers and critics.

Cillian Murphy 's remarkable journey, from humble beginnings to his rise to global stardom. We'll examine his nuanced acting technique, influences, and lasting impact on the cinematic landscape. Join us on a journey into the creative mind of an extraordinary actor who continues to enchant and inspire.

A powerful performance in "Oppenheimer"

In 2023, Cillian Murphy reunited with Christopher Nolan in "Oppenheimer," a biographical film about the life of J. Robert Oppenheimer, the scientist who led the Manhattan Project to develop the atomic bomb. Murphy played the lead role in the film.

Murphy's performance in "Oppenheimer" was praised by critics as one of his best. He played Oppenheimer as a complex and tortured character, caught in the conflict between his scientific genius and the devastating consequences of his creations.

Critics praised the depth and nuance of Murphy's performance, noting his ability to capture Oppenheimer's inner struggles and the weight of responsibility he carried. The film itself has also been acclaimed for its gripping look at history and its lasting ethical implications.

Murphy's performance in "Oppenheimer" further cements his reputation as a top actor capable of portraying complex and fascinating characters. His commitment to authenticity and emotional depth make him an exceptional performer who continues to inspire and captivate audiences.

Stage debut

In September 1996, Cillian Murphy made his grand entrance onto the theater scene in Enda Walsh 's "Disco Pigs ", a play which enjoyed critical and public success. Murphy brilliantly played a rebellious teenager, a performance that revealed his raw talent and magnetic presence.

Her performance was praised by critics for its emotional depth and visceral intensity. Murphy brought the complex character to life with raw vulnerability and explosive energy. Her performance captivated the audience, who were captivated by her natural charisma and unwavering commitment to the role.

Murphy's stage debut in "Disco Pigs " marked a turning point in his career. The play enjoyed a triumphant two-year tour across Europe, Canada and Australia, attracting the attention of film and television directors. This performance paved the way for a successful acting career, leading Murphy to iconic roles on the big and small screen.

Theatrical career of Cillian Murphy

After his notable debut in "Disco Pigs ", Cillian Murphy continued to enrich his theatrical experience by starring in many other acclaimed productions.

In 1998, he played Benedict in an adaptation of Shakespeare's Much Ado About Nothing. Her witty and charming performance delighted audiences and critics alike.

The following year, Murphy starred in "The Country Boy," a moving play about rural life in Ireland. He delivered a poignant and nuanced performance that showcased his ability to embody complex characters.

Also in 1999, Murphy starred in "Juno and the Peacock", a satirical comedy about Irish society. He excellently played the lead role, a proud and headstrong man, bringing unexpected depth and humanity to the character.

These theatrical roles allowed Murphy to explore a wide range of characters and emotions, honing his acting skills and cementing his reputation as one of the most talented performers on the Irish stage.

Film and television debut

Alongside his thriving theater career, Cillian Murphy began exploring the world of film and television.

He appeared in independent films such as "On the Edge " (2001) and short films like " Filleann an Feall " (2000) and " Watchmen " (2001). In 2001, he reprized his role as a teenage rebel in the film adaptation of "Disco Pigs ".

Murphy also made his television debut in the BBC miniseries adaptation "The Way We Live Now ". Her performance in this six-part drama earned her critical acclaim and attracted the attention of movie directors.

In 2001, Murphy moved to London, where he continued to build his acting career. The British capital offered him new opportunities and allowed him to collaborate with internationally renowned filmmakers and actors.

Moving to Hollywood

After proving himself on the Irish and British theater and film scenes, Cillian Murphy attracted the attention of Hollywood directors.

In 2002, while performing in a theater production of Neil LaBute 's "Fausses Appearances" at the Gate Theater in Dublin, Murphy received an offer for a role in the post-apocalyptic horror film "28 Days Later." He jumped at the chance to break into Hollywood.

The move marked a turning point in Murphy's career, opening doors to a wider film scene and allowing him to collaborate with some of the biggest names in the industry.

28 Days Later: The Hollywood Breakthrough

Cillian Murphy 's move to Hollywood quickly paid off when he was cast in the lead role in Danny Boyle's post-apocalyptic horror film "28 Days Later" (2002). Murphy played Jim, a survivor who wakes from a coma in a London hospital to find a world ravaged by a viral rabies outbreak. Disoriented and alone, Jim must fight for survival in a hostile landscape.

Murphy's performance was both moving and terrifying, capturing his character's desperation and determination in the face of overwhelming circumstances. The film was a critical and commercial success, propelling Murphy into the Hollywood spotlight.

After the success of "28 Days Later", Cillian Murphy became a sought-after actor in Hollywood. He continued to star in a variety of roles, from independent films to big-budget blockbusters.

In 2003, he starred alongside Jude Law and Nicole Kidman in the historical drama "Return to Cold Mountain ". His performance as Inman, a Confederate soldier who undertakes a perilous journey to find his lost love, earned him critical praise.

Murphy has also demonstrated his versatility by playing lighter roles, such as in the comedy "Intermission" (2003) and the romantic film " Red Eye " (2005). In the latter, he played the role of a man taken hostage by a mysterious woman during a transatlantic flight.

In 2005, Murphy's breakthrough came when he was cast as Scarecrow in Christopher Nolan's " Dark Knight" trilogy. His portrayal of the iconic villain was both terrifying and tragic, and it cemented his status as one of the most talented and versatile actors of his generation.

Since then, Murphy has continued to star in a wide range of films, including "The Wind Rises" (2006), " Sunshine " (2007), " Inception " (2010) and "Dunkirk" (2017). He also starred in several television series, including " Peaky Blinders " (2013-2022), for which he won two BAFTA Awards for Best Actor.

Today, Cillian Murphy is one of the most respected and in-demand actors in the entertainment industry. His talent, charisma and versatility have allowed him to create an impressive filmography that continues to inspire and captivate audiences.

The discovery of Cillian Murphy

Casting director Gail Stevens was instrumental in discovering Cillian Murphy for the lead role in "28 Days Later." Impressed by her performance in the play "Disco Pigs ", she suggested that Danny Boyle audition her.

It was only after seeing Murphy's slim physique during filming that Boyle and Stevens decided to show him fully nude at the beginning of the film. According to Stevens, Murphy was shy on set, but his dreamy, distant demeanor suited the character perfectly.

Murphy's discovery was a pivotal moment in his career. He brought a raw vulnerability and captivating presence to the role of Jim, which helped make "28 Days Later" a critical and commercial success.

Cillian Murphy 's performance in "28 Days Later" opened many doors for the young actor. He quickly attracted the attention of directors and casting directors around the world, who were impressed by his raw talent and versatility.

In the years since, Murphy has starred in a wide variety of roles, from action heroes to complex villains. He has demonstrated his ability to transform himself physically and emotionally for each role, creating an impressive filmography that is a testament to his immense talent.

One of Murphy's most iconic roles is that of Scarecrow in Christopher Nolan's " Dark Knight" trilogy. His portrayal of the iconic villain was both terrifying and tragic, and it cemented his status as one of the most talented and versatile actors of his generation.

Today, Cillian Murphy continues to be one of the most in-demand actors in Hollywood. He chooses his roles meticulously, seeking projects that challenge him and allow him to explore new facets of his talent. With his ability to portray complex and engaging characters, Murphy will undoubtedly continue to captivate audiences for many years to come.

The impact of "28 Days Later"

The release of "28 Days Later" in 2002 marked a turning point in Cillian Murphy's career and propelled him into the international spotlight. The film quickly became a cult film in North America and a major success worldwide, revealing Murphy's talent to a wide audience.

His performance as Jim earned him nominations for Most Promising Actor at the 8th Annual Empire Awards and Best Male Performance at the MTV Movie Awards. Awards 2004. Murphy praised the film for its depth, considering it much more than just a zombie or horror film.

He expressed surprise at the film's success and the American public's positive reaction to its violent content. For Murphy, "28 Days Later" holds a special place in his heart, as he believes it revolutionized the zombie film genre by introducing fast and agile zombies.

The impact of "28 Days Later" on Murphy's career was undeniable. It opened many doors for the young actor and laid the foundation for his future rise to international stardom.

The rise to international stardom

After the success of "28 Days Later", Cillian Murphy quickly became one of the most in-demand actors in Hollywood. His talent, charisma, and versatility have allowed him to perform in a wide range of roles, from action heroes to complex villains.

He notably played a Confederate soldier in "Return to Cold Mountain " (2003), a young Irish man in "Intermission" (2003) and an FBI agent in " Red Eye " (2005). In 2005, he landed the iconic role of Scarecrow in Christopher Nolan's " Dark Knight" trilogy.

Murphy's portrayal of the Scarecrow was both terrifying and tragic, and it cemented his status as one of the most talented and versatile actors of his generation. He continued to star in critically acclaimed films, such as "The Wind Rises" (2006), " Sunshine " (2007), " Inception " (2010) and "Dunkirk" (2017).

Alongside his film career, Murphy has also starred in several television series, including " Peaky Blinders " (2013-2022), for which he won two BAFTA Awards for Best Actor. Today, Cillian Murphy is one of the most respected and in-demand actors in the entertainment industry. He continues to choose meticulously takes on his roles, seeking out projects that challenge him and allow him to explore new facets of his talent.

Continuation of theatrical and cinematic career

Alongside his rise in Hollywood cinema, Cillian Murphy continued to nurture his passion for acting. In 2003, he played the role of Treplev in a production of Chekhov's "The Seagull" at the Edinburgh International Festival.

The same year, Murphy returned to the big screen in the Irish film "Intermission." He played a unlucky in love and disillusioned supermarket employee who plots a bank robbery alongside Colin Farrell. The film was a commercial success, becoming the highest-grossing Irish independent film in Irish box office history at the time.

These varied roles demonstrated Murphy's versatility as an actor, his ability to move effortlessly from theatrical drama to light comedy and suspense thrillers. His commitment to craft and dedication to bringing complex and endearing characters to life has continued to impress critics and audiences.

Continued success in film and television

After the success of "28 Days Later", "Return to Cold Mountain " and "Intermission", Cillian Murphy has become one of the most sought-after actors in Hollywood. He continued to perform in a variety of roles, demonstrating his versatility and ability to portray complex and endearing characters.

In 2005, Murphy played the pirate Bat Masterson in the western " Red Eye " alongside Rachel McAdams. He also joined the cast of Christopher Nolan's " Dark Knight" trilogy, in which he played the iconic role of the Scarecrow. His terrifying and nuanced performance was praised by critics and has consolidated its status as a leading player.

Alongside his thriving film career, Murphy has also starred in several acclaimed television series. In 2013, he took on the lead role of Tommy Shelby in the British drama series " Peaky Blinders ". His captivating performance as a ruthless yet charismatic gangster earned him numerous awards and helped make the series a worldwide success.

Today, Cillian Murphy continues to be one of the most respected and in-demand actors in the entertainment industry. He chooses his roles meticulously, seeking projects that challenge him and allow him to explore new facets of his talent. With his undeniable charisma, on-screen presence and commitment to excellence, Murphy will undoubtedly continue to captivate audiences for many years to come.

Comparison with Colin Farrell

Cillian Murphy 's performance in "28 Days Later" and "Intermission" led to comparisons to fellow Irishman Colin Farrell. Sarah Lyall of the International Herald Tribune noted that Murphy brought "an ease, a fluidity to the roles he takes on, an intensity that is graceful and entirely believable."

Lyall also commented on Murphy's physical appearance, saying that her "beautiful, delicate appearance" contributed to her attractiveness. However, she noted that Murphy seemed less likely to engage in scandalous behavior, which set him apart from Farrell, who had a reputation as a party animal at the time.

Although Murphy and Farrell are both talented Irish actors, they have followed different career trajectories. Murphy is known for his methodical approach and dedication to his craft, while Farrell is known for his charisma and ability to portray more eccentric characters.

Ultimately, Murphy and Farrell are unique actors with their own strengths and weaknesses. Both men made significant contributions to the Irish and international film industry.

A versatile character actor

Throughout his career, Cillian Murphy has demonstrated his versatility as a character actor, portraying a wide range of characters with depth and authenticity.

From action heroes to complex villains, historical figures to contemporary roles, Murphy brought his talent and commitment to every role he played. His ability to transform himself physically and emotionally for each character is a testament to his commitment to the craft of acting.

Whether as a determined survivor in "28 Days Later," a Civil War soldier in "Return to Cold Mountain," a deranged psychopath in " Red Eye " or the ruthless gangster Tommy Shelby in " Peaky Blinders," Murphy has always managed to captivate audiences with his nuanced and unforgettable performances.

As a character actor, Murphy avoids stereotypical roles and seeks complex and flawed characters. He's not afraid to explore the dark corners of the human soul and bring to life characters who are both appealing and frightening.

Murphy's versatility as a character actor has allowed him to perform in a variety of genres, from historical drama to science fiction to psychological thriller. He has become one of the most respected and in-demand actors of his generation, and his performances continue to entertain and inspire audiences around the world.

Significant secondary roles

Although Cillian Murphy is best known for his starring roles in hit films like "28 Days Later" and " Peaky Blinders ", he also played memorable supporting roles throughout his career.

In the historical drama "Return to Cold Mountain " (2003), Murphy played a soldier shot in the back by Natalie Portman 's character. Despite his relatively minor role, Murphy left a lasting impression with his poignant performance. He praised director Anthony Minghella for his calm and professionalism on set.

Murphy also played a butcher in "Girl with a Pearl Earring" (2003), a historical drama starring Scarlett Johansson and Colin Firth. Although it was a supporting role, Murphy brought his charisma and screen presence, creating a memorable character despite his limited screen time.

These supporting roles allowed Murphy to demonstrate his versatility as an actor, his ability to portray varied characters with depth and credibility. They also helped cement his reputation as a talented and reliable actor, capable of stealing the show in even the most modest roles.

Return to the stage with the Druid Theater Company

In 2004, Cillian Murphy returned to the stage with the Druid Theater Company, a renowned Irish theater company. He joined an Irish tour of JM Synge's "The Playboy of the Western World", playing the lead role of Christy Mahon.

The production was directed by Garry Hynes, who had previously directed Murphy in " Juno and the Paycock " in 1999. Murphy also reprized his role as Tim Murphy in "The Country Boy" during this tour.

These performances allowed Murphy to reconnect with his theatrical roots and perform for Irish audiences. They also testified to his continued commitment to theater, despite his growing success in the film industry.

"The Playboy of the Western World" tour received rave reviews, with critics praising Murphy's performance as Christy Mahon. Her performance was both sensitive and powerful, capturing the vulnerability and complexity of the character.

This experience reminded Murphy of the importance of theater in his life and reinforced his love for the stage. He continues to support the Druid Theater Company and occasionally participate in theatrical productions.

Become the Scarecrow in "Batman Begins "

In 2005, Cillian Murphy joined the cast of "Batman Begins ", Christopher Nolan's film about the origins of the iconic superhero. Initially, Murphy was contacted to audition for the role of Bruce Wayne/Batman. However, he believed he did not have the imposing physique necessary to play the Dark Knight.

Still, Murphy decided to meet Nolan, and the director was so impressed by the actor's presence and talent that he offered him the role of supervillain Dr. Jonathan Crane/Scarecrow.

Murphy took this opportunity and brought his own unique interpretation to the character. His Scarecrow was both frightening and tragic, a man broken by his own fears and his obsession with psychological manipulation.

Murphy's performance in "Batman Begins " received critical acclaim, and his Scarecrow became one of the Batman franchise's most memorable villains. He reprized the role in the sequels "The Dark Knight" (2008) and "The Dark Knight Rises " (2012), completing his trilogy as Dr. Crane.

Murphy's experience in "Batman Begins " was a pivotal moment in his career, helping him reach a wider audience and cement his status as an A-list actor.

Pursuit of terror in the " Dark Knight" trilogy

After playing Scarecrow in "Batman Begins ", Cillian Murphy reprized the role in the sequels "The Dark Knight" (2008) and "The Dark Knight Rises " (2012). His portrayal of the iconic villain remained both unsettling and captivating throughout the trilogy.

In "The Dark Knight," Scarecrow teams up with the even more chaotic Joker to spread fear and confusion in Gotham City. Murphy brought additional nuance to the character, exploring his complex relationship with Batman and his own motivations.

In "The Dark Knight Rises ", Scarecrow plays a central role in Bane's plan to destroy Gotham. Murphy portrayed the character's terror and despair as he is subjected to the Joker's fear toxins and forced to confront his own demons.

Murphy's performance in the " Dark Knight" trilogy cemented his status as one of the most talented and versatile actors of his generation. His Scarecrow has become an iconic villain in Batman history, and his contribution to the franchise remains highly regarded by fans.

A perfect villain in " Red Eye "

In 2005, Murphy played a different role in the thriller " Red Eye " by Wes Craven. He played Jackson Rippner, a terrorist who takes an FBI agent (Rachel McAdams) hostage during a nighttime robbery.

Manohla Dargis of The New York Times praised Murphy's performance, calling him "the perfect villain". She noted that his "blue eyes were cold enough to freeze water" and that his "wolf-like gaze suggested his own terrors."

" Red Eye " received favorable reviews and was a commercial success, grossing nearly $100 million worldwide. Mu rphy's performance as a manipulative psychopath demonstrated his ability to play roles that were both frightening and endearing.

A versatile character actor

Throughout his career, Cillian Murphy has demonstrated his versatility as a character actor, portraying a wide range of characters with depth and authenticity.

From action heroes to complex villains, historical figures to contemporary roles, Murphy brought his talent and commitment to every role he played. His ability to transform himself physically and emotionally for each character is a testament to his commitment to the craft of acting.

Whether as a determined survivor in "28 Days Later," a Civil War soldier in "Return to Cold Mountain," a deranged psychopath in " Red Eye " or the ruthless gangster Tommy Shelby in " Peaky Blinders," Murphy has always managed to captivate audiences with his nuanced and unforgettable performances.

As a character actor, Murphy avoids stereotypical roles and seeks complex and flawed characters. He 's not afraid to explore the dark corners of the human soul and bring to life characters who are both appealing and frightening.

Murphy's versatility as a character actor has allowed him to perform in a variety of genres, from historical drama to science fiction to psychological thriller. He has become one of the most respected and in-demand actors of his generation, and his performances continue to entertain and inspire audiences around the world.

Recognition for villain roles

Cillian Murphy 's performances in "Batman Begins " and " Red" Eye " in 2005 earned him critical acclaim and nominations for his villainous roles.

He was nominated for Best Villain at the MTV Movie Awards. Awards 2006 for his portrayal of Scarecrow in "Batman Begins ". Entertainment Weekly listed him as one of the best actors of summer 2005 for his roles in "Batman Begins " and " Red Eye."

David Denby of The New Yorker praised Murphy's performance in " Red Eye ", writing: " Cillian Murphy, who has an angelic demeanor that can turn sinister, is one of the most elegantly seductive monsters in recent films."

These nominations and accolades were a testament to Murphy's ability to portray evil characters with complexity and credibility. His performances left a lasting impression on audiences and helped solidify his reputation as a talented and versatile actor.

An acclaimed and respected actor

Over the years, Cillian Murphy has received numerous nominations and awards for his outstanding on-screen performances.

In 2006, he was nominated for a Golden Globe for Best Actor in a Motion Picture Musical or Comedy for his role in "Breakfast on Pluto ". He also won two Irish Film and Television Awards for Best Actor for his roles in "Breakfast on Pluto " and "The Wind Rises".

In 2017 and 2018, Murphy won two British Academy Television Awards for Best Actor for his role as Tommy Shelby in the television series " Peaky Blinders ". It also won an Irish Film and Television Award for Best Actor in a Television Drama for his role in " Peaky Blinders " in 2018.

These awards and nominations are a testament to Murphy's talent, versatility and commitment to the craft of acting. He is recognized as one of the most talented and respected actors of his generation, and his work continues to inspire and entertain audiences around the world.

Nuanced interpretation in "Breakfast on Pluto "

In 2005, Cillian Murphy delivered an extraordinary performance in "Breakfast on Pluto ", a comedy-drama by Neil Jordan based on the novel of the same title by Patrick McCabe.

Murphy played Patrick Braden, aka Kitten, a transgender Irish woman who goes looking for her mother. The film explores Kitten 's journey through the 1970s, as she navigates a complex world of glam rock, red light districts and IRA violence.

Murphy brought exceptional depth and nuance to the character of Kitten. He captured Kitten 's vulnerability and resilience as she struggles to find her identity and place in the world. Murphy's performance received critical acclaim, and he was nominated for a Golden Globe for Best Actor in a Motion Picture Musical or Comedy for his role.

"Breakfast on Pluto " was a critical and commercial success, and Murphy's performance was recognized as one of his best roles. The film explored important themes such as identity, acceptance, and finding one's roots, and Murphy's performance helped bring these themes to life with sensitivity and humanity.

A committed and versatile actor

Throughout his career, Cillian Murphy has demonstrated an unwavering commitment to the craft of acting and remarkable versatility in his roles.

He has played a wide range of characters, from action heroes to complex villains, from historical figures to contemporary roles, with depth and authenticity. Her ability to transform herself physically and emotionally for each character is a testament to her dedication to her craft.

Whether as a determined survivor in "28 Days Later," a Civil War soldier in "Return to Cold Mountain," a deranged psychopath in " Red Eye " or the ruthless gangster Tommy Shelby in " Peaky Blinders," Murphy has always managed to captivate audiences with his nuanced and unforgettable performances.

Murphy's commitment to excellence is reflected in the numerous nominations and awards he has received for his work. He was nominated for a Golden Globe, won two British Academy

Television Awards and received several Irish Film and Television Awards.

Cillian Murphy is an exceptional actor whose talent and versatility continue to inspire and entertain audiences around the world.

Determination to play Kitten in "Breakfast on Pluto "

Cillian Murphy was determined to play Patrick Braden / Kitten in "Breakfast on Pluto ", despite director Neil Jordan's initial hesitation.

Murphy had auditioned for the role in 2001, and Jordan wanted to give it to him. However, Jordan was reluctant to revisit the themes of transgender people and the IRA, which were central to the film.

Murphy lobbied Jordan for several years to direct the film before he was too old for the role. In 2004, he began preparing for the role by meeting a transvestite with whom he crossdressed and went to clubs.

The role required waxing of his eyebrows, chest and legs, which Murphy did with dedication. His extensive preparation and determination to play the role ultimately convinced Jordan to direct the film.

Murphy's performance in "Breakfast on Pluto " received critical acclaim, and he was nominated for a Golden Globe for his role. The film explored important themes such as identity, acceptance, and finding one's roots, and Murphy's performance helped bring these themes to life with sensitivity and humanity.

A committed and passionate artist

Cillian Murphy 's determination to play Kitten in "Breakfast on Pluto " is a testament to his commitment to his craft and his passion for telling important stories.

His willingness to prepare meticulously for the role, both physically and emotionally, demonstrates his dedication to the craft of acting. His ability to bring complex and flawed characters to life reflects his depth as an artist.

Murphy's performance in "Breakfast on Pluto " raised awareness about issues of gender and identity, and helped destigmatize the experiences of transgender people. His work continues to inspire and educate audiences, and his commitment to meaningful cinema is an inspiration to aspiring actors and filmmakers.

As a committed and passionate artist, Cillian Murphy uses his talent and platform to tell thought-provoking stories that have a lasting impact on the world.

Critical reception of Murphy's performance

Cillian Murphy 's performance in "Breakfast on Pluto " received widespread critical acclaim.

Roger Ebert noted how Murphy played the character with a "perplexed, hopeful voice ". Even the film's mixed reviews praised Murphy's performance.

However, a few reviewers have expressed differing opinions. The Village Voice found the film "unconvincing" and too cute.

Despite these criticisms, Murphy's performance has been recognized as one of the film's strong points. Her ability to embody Kitten 's vulnerability and strength was praised, and her performance helped bring the film's touching and complex story to life.

A versatile and acclaimed actor

Cillian Murphy is a versatile and acclaimed actor whose talent and commitment are reflected in his wide range of roles.

His performance in "Breakfast on Pluto " demonstrates his ability to portray complex and flawed characters with depth and authenticity. His other notable roles include the determined survivor in "28 Days Later", the Civil War soldier in "Return to Cold Mountain ", the troubled psychologist in " Red Eye " and the ruthless gangster Tommy Shelby in " Peaky Blinders ".

Murphy's nuanced and unforgettable performances have earned him numerous nominations and awards, including a Golden Globe nomination and two British Academy Awards. Television Awards. He is recognized as one of the most talented and respected actors of his generation, and his work continues to inspire and entertain audiences around the world.

Recognition and praise for the performance in "Breakfast on Pluto "

Cillian Murphy 's performance in "Breakfast on Pluto " earned him numerous nominations and accolades.

He was nominated for a Golden Globe Award for Best Actor in a Musical or Comedy for his role, a testament to the recognition of his nuanced and touching performance.

Additionally, Murphy won a fourth Best Actor award from the Irish Film and Television Academy. This award recognizes his continued commitment to Irish cinema and his excellence in this complex role.

The French magazine Première included Murphy's performance in its top 24 best performances of 2005. This highlights the international impact of his work and his ability to captivate audiences around the world.

These nominations and awards are a tribute to Murphy's immense talent and dedication as an actor. His performance in "Breakfast on Pluto " remains a testament to his ability to bring unforgettable characters to life and explore important themes with sensitivity and humanity.

A leading actor

Cillian Murphy 's acclaimed performances in "Breakfast on Pluto " and countless other roles have cemented his position as a leading actor in the film industry.

His ability to portray a wide range of characters with depth and authenticity has made him one of the most sought-after and respected actors of his generation. His nuanced and unforgettable performances have captivated audiences around the world and earned him numerous nominations and awards.

Whether as an action hero, complex villain, historical figure, or contemporary role, Murphy always brings a level of skill and dedication to his work that is unmatched. He is a master of transformation, able to slip into the skin of any character and bring them to life with remarkable humanity and depth.

Murphy's unwavering commitment to the craft of acting and his exceptional talent make him a true artist whose work continues to inspire and entertain audiences around the world.

A deep connection with "The Wind Rises"

Cillian Murphy 's connection to the film "The Wind Rises" was deeply personal. Growing up near Cork, Ireland, where the film was filmed, Murphy had intimate knowledge of the historical events that formed the story.

His connection to the city gave him a sense of responsibility in his portrayal of Damien O'Donovan, a young doctor turned revolutionary. He auditioned for the role six times before getting it, a testament to his dedication to portraying the character authentically.

For Murphy, the film was not only a cinematic project, but also an opportunity to explore his own heritage and pay tribute to those who fought for Irish independence. He said he was "extremely proud" of the film, noting that "the memories dig very deep - the politics, the divisions and everyone has stories of family members who were caught up in the struggle."

Murphy's performance in "The Wind Rises" was infused with this deep understanding of the subject. He brought raw emotion and intensity to his role, portraying the struggles and sacrifices of the Irish revolutionaries with remarkable sensitivity and depth.

An ambassador of Irish cinema

Cillian Murphy is not only an exceptional actor, but also a passionate ambassador for Irish cinema. His involvement in films such as "The Wind Rises" demonstrates his commitment to supporting and promoting his country's film industry.

By starring in Irish films and collaborating with Irish filmmakers, Murphy helps to increase the visibility and recognition of Irish cinema on the international scene. He is an inspiration to aspiring Irish actors and filmmakers, demonstrating that it is possible to achieve excellence in the film industry while remaining true to your roots.

Murphy's commitment to Irish cinema extends beyond his own acting work. He is also a strong supporter of organizations and initiatives that support and promote Irish cinema. His involvement in the Irish film community demonstrates his deep love for his country and his desire to support its culture and heritage.

Critical praise

Cillian Murphy 's performance in "The Wind Rises" was praised by critics, who highlighted his ability to capture the complexity of his character.

David Denby noted Murphy's moments of profound stillness and idiosyncrasy in his portrayal of Damien O'Donovan. Kenneth Turan of the Los Angeles Times wrote: " Cillian Murphy is particularly good at playing fanaticism as well as introspection and regret, to show us a man who is eaten alive because he is forced to act in a manner which is contrary to his background and his training."

In recognition of his outstanding performance, Murphy was awarded the 2006 Actor of the Year award by GQ UK for his work in "The Wind Rises". These accolades are a testament to Murphy's exceptional talent and ability to bring complex and compelling characters to life.

Cillian Murphy is a versatile and acclaimed actor whose talent and commitment are reflected in his wide range of roles.

Her performance in "The Wind Rises" demonstrates her ability to portray complex and flawed characters with depth and authenticity. His other notable roles include the determined survivor in "28 Days Later", the Civil War soldier in "Return to Cold Mountain ", the deranged psychopath in " Red Eye " and the ruthless gangster Tommy Shelby in " Peaky Blinders."

Murphy's nuanced and unforgettable performances have earned him numerous nominations and awards, including a Golden Globe nomination and two British Academy Awards. Television Awards. He is recognized as one of the most talented and respected actors of his generation, and his work continues to inspire and entertain audiences around the world.

Return to stage in "Love Song"

In 2006, Cillian Murphy returned to the stage at the New Ambassadors Theater in London's West End, alongside Neve Campbell, in the play "Love Song" by John Kolvenbach.

Murphy played the lead role of Beane, a "sentimental loner hero", "jovially grumpy" and "mentally unstable", according to Theater Record. Variety praised her performance, calling it "as magnetic on stage as on screen", noting that her "unhurried bewilderment strips away the slight preciousness from the brothel character's mad-scientist naivete".

This performance demonstrated Murphy's versatility as an actor, his ability to successfully portray complex and endearing characters, both on the big screen and on stage.

An accomplished stage actor

In addition to his on-screen success, Cillian Murphy is also an accomplished stage actor. His stage performances have been critically acclaimed for their depth, nuance and intensity.

Her roles in plays such as "Disco Pigs ", "Love Song" and "The Playboy of the Western World" showcased her ability to bring complex characters to life and explore universal human themes of love, of loss and redemption.

Murphy's commitment to theater speaks to his passion for the craft of acting and his desire to connect with audiences on a more intimate level. His stage performances continue to inspire and captivate audiences, cementing his reputation as a versatile and talented artist.

Ongoing collaborations and new roles

After the success of "28 Days Later", Cillian Murphy continued to collaborate with director Danny Boyle in the science fiction film " Sunshine " (2007). He played a physicist-astronaut tasked with rekindling the sun.

Murphy also explored lighter roles in the romantic comedy " Watching the Detectives " (2007), where he starred alongside Lucy Liu. Additionally, he was cast as Richard Neville, the editor of the radical psychedelic underground magazine Oz, in the film "Hippie Hippie Shake " (2007). However, this project was delayed and ultimately abandoned in 2011.

These varied roles demonstrated Murphy's versatility as an actor, his ability to move effortlessly between different genres and characters. His commitment to playing complex and challenging roles has continued to attract the attention of renowned filmmakers and audiences around the world.

Career progression and recognition

Throughout his career, Cillian Murphy has demonstrated an unwavering commitment to the craft of acting. Her nuanced and unforgettable performances in a wide range of roles have earned Murphy numerous prestigious nominations and awards.

Nominations at the Golden Globes and the British Academy Television Irish Film and Television Awards Awards, Murphy's recognition by the film industry is a testament to his exceptional talent and significant contribution to the art of cinema and television.

Murphy's versatility, dedication to his craft, and ability to portray complex and endearing characters have cemented his reputation as an elite actor. His work continues to inspire and entertain audiences around the world, raising the level of the entertainment industry and leaving a lasting legacy in the world of cinema.

Continued success in cinema

In 2008, Cillian Murphy reprized the iconic role of Scarecrow in "The Dark Knight", the highly anticipated sequel to "Batman Begins ". His terrifying and nuanced performance helped make the film a critical and commercial success.

Murphy also starred in the romantic film "The Edge of Love," which explored the life and work of poet Dylan Thomas. He shared the bill with Keira Knightley, Sienna Miller and Matthew Rhys.

Additionally, An Post honored Murphy by issuing a stamp with his image, recognizing his contribution to the Irish film industry. This honor was a testament to Murphy's impact on the Irish film landscape and his position as one of the country's most talented and recognized actors.

Throughout his career, Cillian Murphy has demonstrated remarkable versatility, successfully portraying a wide range of characters in genres ranging from drama to thriller to science fiction.

His nuanced and moving performances have captivated audiences around the world, earning him critical and commercial recognition. From iconic roles like Scarecrow in the " Dark Knight" trilogy to complex characters in independent films such as "Breakfast on Pluto," Murphy has proven his exceptional acting talent time and time again.

Whether on the big screen, stage or television, Murphy brings a level of engagement and authenticity to every role he plays. His dedication to the craft of acting and his ability to bring unforgettable characters to life have cemented his reputation as a leading actor in the entertainment industry.

Exploration of new artistic territories

In 2009, Cillian Murphy ventured into new artistic territories by starring in the Canadian short film "The Water", directed by Kevin Drew of the rock band Broken Social Scene.

Murphy, himself a fan of Broken Social Scene, was attracted to the role because of the almost silent nature of the film. He considered silent films "the toughest test for any actor", and the opportunity allowed him to push his creative limits.

Murphy also starred in " Perrier's Bounty," a crime comedy from the writers of "Intermission." He played a small-time criminal on the run from a gangster played by Brendan Gleeson.

These varied roles demonstrated Murphy's versatility as an actor, his ability to effortlessly move between different genres and portray complex and endearing characters. His commitment to exploring new artistic territories speaks to his passion for the craft of acting and his constant desire to take on creative challenges.

evolving player

Throughout his career, Cillian Murphy has demonstrated a constant desire to evolve and reinvent himself as an actor. He has continued to explore new genres, tackle complex roles and collaborate with talented directors.

Whether playing a petty criminal in a crime comedy or bringing a mute character to life in an experimental short film, Murphy brings a level of engagement and authenticity to every performance. His ability to transform himself physically and emotionally for each role is a testament to his dedication to the craft of acting.

Murphy's constant evolution as an actor is a testament to his exceptional talent and passion for his craft. He is an artist who refuses to rest on his laurels and who always seeks to push his creative limits.

Return to the stage and exploration of new genres

In 2010, Cillian Murphy returned to the stage as part of ' From Galway to Broadway and back again ', a show celebrating the 35th anniversary of the Druid Theater Company.

Alongside his theater commitments, Murphy continued to explore new genres on screen. He starred in the direct-to-video psychological thriller Peacock 's Secret alongside Elliot Page, Susan Sarandon and Bill Pullman.

In this film, Murphy played a man with a split personality who makes people believe that he is also his own wife. This complex and challenging role allowed Murphy to demonstrate his ability to explore the darkest corners of the human psyche.

Murphy's versatility as an actor and his willingness to take on bold, challenging roles have continued to impress critics and audiences. His commitment to pushing his creative boundaries and bringing complex, memorable characters to life has cemented his reputation as a leading actor.

Continued collaboration with Christopher Nolan

In 2010, Cillian Murphy reunited with director Christopher Nolan for the sci-fi thriller film " Inception." He played an entrepreneur whose mind is infiltrated by the character played by Leonardo DiCaprio, who tries to convince him to dissolve his company.

This complex and challenging role allowed Murphy to demonstrate his ability to portray vulnerable and flawed characters. Her performance was praised by critics, who noted her ability to bring depth and nuance to a character struggling with inner conflicts and moral dilemmas.

In the same year, Murphy made an uncredited appearance in " Tron : Legacy", the sequel to the classic science fiction film " Tron ". He played Edward Dillinger Jr., the son of the main antagonist of the original film.

These roles were a testament to Murphy's versatility as an actor and his ability to effortlessly transition between different genres. His continued collaboration with leading directors like Christopher Nolan has cemented his reputation as a leading actor and allowed him to explore complex and challenging characters on the big screen.

Triumph on stage in " Misterman "

In 2011, Cillian Murphy returned to the stage in the acclaimed play " Misterman ", written and directed by Enda Walsh, his long-time collaborator on "Disco Pigs ".

" Misterman " was performed in Galway, Ireland before touring to Saint Ann's Warehouse in Brooklyn, New York. Murphy played the title role, a man who struggles with loneliness and isolation in an alienating modern world.

Murphy's performance was praised by critics, who praised his ability to capture his character's vulnerability and angst. It won the Irish Times Theater Award and a Drama Desk Award for his outstanding performance.

Murphy's success in " Misterman " cemented his reputation as an accomplished stage actor. His ability to bring complex and emotional characters to life on stage has continued to impress critics and audiences, demonstrating his versatility as a performer.

A captivating performance in " Misterman "

Cillian Murphy 's performance in " Misterman " was praised by critics for its depth and nuance. Sarah Lyall of the International Herald Tribune described his character, Thomas Magill, as "a complicated mix of sympathetic and utterly unsympathetic – deeply wounded with a moral code, but dangerous and biased."

Lyall noted Murphy's "unusual ability to create and inhabit frightening yet compelling characters from the big screen to the small stage in the intensely staged single Misterman ". She also spoke of the audience's powerful reaction to her performance, noting that one evening "the theater was flooded, not with applause but with silence" which culminated in a standing ovation.

Lyall 's praise is a testament to Murphy's ability to portray complex and flawed characters with remarkable depth and emotional resonance. His performance in " Misterman " not only captivated audiences, but also earned him critical acclaim, cementing his reputation as an exceptionally talented stage actor.

Throughout his career, Cillian Murphy has established himself as a dedicated and versatile artist, capable of bringing a wide range of characters to life on stage and screen with depth and authenticity.

His acclaimed performance in " Misterman " is a testament to his commitment to acting craft and his ability to explore the darkest corners of the human psyche. Murphy isn't afraid to take creative risks and embody complex and flawed characters, allowing the audience to connect with them on a deep level.

Whether in blockbuster films, intimate plays, or gripping television series, Murphy always brings remarkable intensity and depth to his performances. His dedication to his craft and his ability to bring unforgettable characters to life have made him one of the most respected and in-demand actors of his generation.

Continued genre exploration in " Retreat " and "Time Out"

After the success of " Misterman ", Cillian Murphy continued to explore different film genres with roles in " Retreat " and "Time Out".

In the British horror film " Retreat ", Murphy played the lead role of a man vacationing with his wife on a remote island, where they face sinister forces. Although the film had a limited release, Murphy's performance was praised for its intensity and believability.

In "Time Out", a science fiction film starring Justin Timberlake and Amanda Seyfried, Murphy played a supporting role. Despite mixed reviews, Murphy's performance was noted for its depth and nuance, demonstrating his ability to elevate even the most minor roles.

Despite the mixed critical reception of these films, Murphy's commitment to portraying complex and challenging characters remained evident. His willingness to explore different genres and collaborate with diverse filmmakers has been a testament to his passion for the craft of acting and his continued search for creative challenges.

Exciting new collaborations and roles

In 2012, Cillian Murphy collaborated with two Hollywood legends, Robert De Niro and Sigourney Weaver, in the supernatural thriller " Red Lights." He played Tom Buckley, the assistant to a paranormal investigator played by Weaver.

Although the film received mixed reviews, Murphy's performance was praised for its depth and nuance. He also reprized his iconic role as the Scarecrow in "The Dark Knight Rises ", concluding the " Dark Knight" trilogy with intensity and menace.

In the British independent film " Broken ", Murphy played a supporting role as Mike, the main character's favorite teacher. His performance earned him a British Independent Film Award nomination for Best Supporting Actor, testament to his ability to elevate even the smallest roles with his intensity and authenticity.

These collaborations and varied roles demonstrated Murphy's versatility as an actor and his commitment to portraying complex and challenging characters.

Throughout his career, Cillian Murphy has demonstrated a constant desire to evolve and reinvent himself as an actor. He has explored a wide range of characters and genres, from action heroes to complex villains, from historical figures to contemporary roles.

Whether on the big screen, stage or television, Murphy brings a level of engagement and authenticity to every role he plays. His dedication to the craft of acting and his ability to bring unforgettable characters to life have cemented his reputation as a leading actor in the entertainment industry.

Murphy's constant evolution as an actor is a testament to his exceptional talent and passion for his craft. He is an artist who refuses to rest on his laurels and who always seeks to push his creative limits.

The international success of " Peaky Blinders "

From 2013 to 2022, Cillian Murphy played the lead role of Tommy Shelby in the hit BBC television series Peaky Blinders ". The series follows the journey of a criminal gang in post-World War I England.

Murphy's outstanding performance as Tommy Shelby, a charismatic and ruthless gang leader, was praised by critics and audiences. The series has become an international phenomenon, captivating viewers with its gripping storyline, complex characters and evocative atmosphere.

The role of Tommy Shelby allowed Murphy to demonstrate his versatility as an actor. He brought to life a character both fascinating and frightening, capable of extreme violence and fierce loyalty. Murphy's performance earned " Peaky Blinders " numerous awards, including the British Academy Television Award for Best Drama Series and the Golden Globe Award for Best Television Series, Drama.

The success of " Peaky Blinders " cemented Murphy's reputation as one of the most talented and respected actors of his generation. The series not only captivated audiences, but also allowed Murphy to explore important social and historical themes, such as war trauma, organized crime and working class struggles.

A lasting cultural impact

" Peaky Blinders " became more than just a successful television series; it had a lasting cultural impact. The fashion, music and lifestyle of the era depicted in the series saw a resurgence in popularity. The series also drew attention to the history of Birmingham and the English Midlands, highlighting their rich industrial past and unique culture.

Cillian Murphy 's performance as Tommy Shelby played a key role in the success and impact of " Peaky Blinders ". His nuanced and powerful portrayal of a complex and fascinating character captivated audiences and left an indelible mark on the world of television.

Peaky 's Legacy Blinders " lives on through its numerous awards, international success and lasting cultural influence. The series remains a testament to Cillian Murphy's exceptional talent and ability to bring to life unforgettable characters that resonate deeply with audiences.

Critical recognition and public success

" Peaky Blinders " has received critical acclaim for its gripping storyline, complex characters and exceptional performances. The series has won numerous awards, including the British Academy Television Award for Best Drama Series and the Golden Globe Award for Best Television Series, Drama.

In addition to critical acclaim, " Peaky Blinders " enjoyed immense public success. The series became an international phenomenon, with fans around the world captivated by the story of the Birmingham criminal gang. The success of the series cemented Cillian Murphy 's reputation as the one of the most talented and respected actors of his generation.

In 2013, Murphy made his directorial debut with the music video for " Hold Me Forever ", a single by the band Money. The video featured dancers from the English National Ballet and was filmed at the Old Vic Theater in London. Murphy's directorial debut was praised for its creativity and artistic vision.

The continued success of " Peaky Blinders " and Murphy's promising directorial debut are a testament to his versatility as an artist. He is not only an exceptional actor, but also a creative visionary with a unique ability to captivate audiences.

Collaborations with renowned talents

In 2014, Cillian Murphy co-starred with Jennifer Connelly in the drama "The Dreamcatcher." He also starred in Wally Pfister 's "Transcendence", alongside Johnny Depp and Rebecca Hall.

These collaborations with renowned talents allowed Murphy to demonstrate his versatility as an actor. He brought to life a wide range of characters, from the man haunted by his memories in "The Dreamcatcher" to the scientist obsessed with immortality in "Transcendence."

Murphy also reconnected with Enda Walsh, his long-time collaborator from "Disco Pigs " and " Misterman ", for the play " Ballyturk ". The play explored themes of identity, loss and redemption in rural Ireland.

Murphy's willingness to work with talented filmmakers and playwrights is a testament to his commitment to the craft of acting. He is always looking for new creative challenges and collaborations that push his artistic boundaries.

A foray into blockbuster and musical exploration

In 2015, Cillian Murphy starred in Ron Howard's hit film "In the Heart of the Sea", alongside Benjamin Walker and Chris Hemsworth. He also contributed his speaking vocals to the tracks "8:58" and "The Clock " from Paul Hartnoll 's album "8:58".

"In the Heart of the Ocean" was an adventure blockbuster based on the true story of the crew of the whaler Essex, who were attacked by a giant sperm whale. Murphy's role in the film was that of Matthew Joy, an experienced sailor struggling to survive in the unforgiving wilderness.

Murphy's collaboration with Paul Hartnoll on "8:58" marked his first foray into music. He brought his distinctive speaking voice to the album's tracks, creating a dark, evocative atmosphere that perfectly complemented Hartnoll 's electronic music.

Murphy's versatility as an artist is evident in his role choices and creative collaborations. He is able to effortlessly move from blockbuster to musical experimentation, bringing his talent and dedication to every project he undertakes.

A heartbreaking performance in " Anthropoid "

In 2016, Cillian Murphy starred in " Anthropoid ", a film about Operation Anthropoid, a World War II mission that aimed to assassinate Reinhard Heydrich, a high-ranking Nazi official. Murphy played Jozef Gabčík, a Czechoslovakian soldier who was one of two men assigned to carry out the mission.

Murphy's performance in " Anthropoid " was heartbreaking. It brought to life the complexity and internal conflict of Gabčík, a man torn between his duty to his country and the personal costs of war. The film was praised by critics for its gripping realism and moving portrait of the Czech resistance.

Murphy's performance in " Anthropoid " once again demonstrated his ability to portray complex historical figures and explore themes of war, identity and sacrifice. His commitment to authenticity and attention to detail made " Anthropoid " a powerful and moving film.

Capturing the trauma of war in "Dunkirk"

In 2017, Cillian Murphy starred in Christopher Nolan's war film "Dunkirk". He plays an army officer who is the victim of shell shock, a psychological condition caused by exposure to explosions. Murphy's character has no name and is simply referred to as a "shivering soldier".

Murphy approached this role with great sensitivity and a deep understanding of the psychological impact of war. He said his character was "representative of something experienced by thousands of soldiers, the heavy emotional and psychological toll that war can take."

Murphy's performance in "Dunkirk" was understated and moving. He captured his character's trauma and vulnerability with remarkable authenticity. The film received critical acclaim for its immersive intensity and poignant tribute to the soldiers who fought at Dunkirk.

Murphy's performance in "Dunkirk" once again demonstrated his commitment to complex and challenging roles. He is able to bring to life the stories of characters who have undergone profound and often traumatic experiences, bringing humanity and understanding to complex historical events.

A discreet personal life and a fulfilled family

Cillian Murphy has been married to artist and producer Yvonne McGuinness since 2004. They met in 1996 at one of Murphy's rock band The Sons of Mr. Green Genes' concerts.

The couple is known for their privacy and are fiercely protective of their family life. They live in Dublin with their two sons, Malachy and Aran. Murphy said being a father has given him a new meaning in life and he cherishes time spent with his family.

Murphy's personal life is in stark contrast to his often intense and troubled on-screen roles. He is described as a devoted father and husband, as well as a loyal and supportive friend. His balance between a successful career and a fulfilling family life is a testament to his integrity and priorities.

A harmonious balance

Cillian Murphy has managed to find a harmonious balance between his professional and personal life. Although he is an in-demand actor, he prioritizes his family and private life.

His ability to separate his professional and personal life is a testament to his maturity and emotional intelligence. He understands the importance of maintaining clear boundaries to preserve his well-being and that of his family.

By fiercely protecting his privacy, Murphy protects his safe, intimate space, where he can recharge and reconnect with his loved ones. This allows him to return to his work with a fresh perspective and renewed energy, which contributes to his exceptional on-screen performances.

Murphy's harmonious balance between her career and personal life is an example to others on how to live a fulfilling and satisfying life, both professionally and personally.

Music, vegetarianism and running: other sides of Murphy

Besides his passion for music, Cillian Murphy is also interested in other areas. For many years he was a vegetarian, not out of moral opposition to meat-eating, but because of his concerns about unhealthy agricultural practices. However, he resumed eating meat for his role in " Peaky Blinders."

Murphy is also an experienced runner, which allows him to maintain peak fitness and let off some steam.

These lesser-known facets of Murphy reveal a well-rounded and passionate individual who balances his acting work with his personal interests. His curiosity and willingness to explore new experiences contribute to his growth as an artist and his ability to portray complex and believable characters on screen.

A multi-faceted artist

Cillian Murphy is a multi-faceted artist whose interests extend beyond performance. His passion for music, his vegetarian journey and his love of running demonstrate his curiosity and desire to explore different aspects of life.

These facets of Murphy's life enrich his work as an actor by providing him with a broader perspective on the world and a deeper understanding of the human condition. They also allow him to connect with a wider audience who share his interests and values.

By embracing these different facets, Murphy demonstrates that one can lead a fulfilling and balanced life while pursuing a successful artistic career. He serves as an example to others on how to cultivate their passions and find meaning in various aspects of their lives.

Food awareness and fitness

Food consciousness and fitness are important aspects of Cillian Murphy's life.

As a lifelong vegetarian, Murphy refrained from consuming meat due to his concerns about unhealthy agricultural practices. However, he resumed eating meat for his role in " Peaky Blinders," demonstrating his willingness to transform himself physically and mentally for his roles.

Aside from his diet, Murphy is also a seasoned runner. He regularly runs to maintain his physical shape and to let off steam. His passion for running highlights the importance he places on health and well-being.

Murphy's food consciousness and fitness are personal choices that reflect his values and commitment to living a healthy, balanced life. They also testify to his discipline and determination, essential qualities for an actor who wishes to embody credible and authentic characters.

Private life and connection with Ireland

Cillian Murphy is deeply connected to his hometown and home country of Ireland. He chose to live and work in nearby

Dublin, avoiding the move to Hollywood despite his international fame.

Murphy is known for his private life, preferring to keep his family and personal life out of the public eye. He rarely made appearances on live television chat shows, favoring more intimate and controlled interviews.

This approach reflects the value Murphy places on authenticity and privacy. He wants his work to speak for itself, rather than engaging in self-promotion or exposure of his personal life. By staying close to his roots and protecting his privacy, Murphy maintains a healthy balance between his acting career and his personal well-being.

A humble and centered artist

Cillian Murphy 's humility and centeredness are essential qualities that guide his life and career.

Despite his success and worldwide recognition, Murphy remains humble and grateful for the opportunities he has been given. He doesn't take himself too seriously and maintains a strong connection with his community and those close to him.

Murphy's centeredness allows him to stay grounded in the present moment and focus on the work that really matters. He avoids the distractions and glitz of Hollywood, preferring to focus on creating authentic and meaningful performances.

Murphy's humility and centeredness are an inspiration to other actors and artists. They demonstrate that you can succeed in the entertainment industry without losing sight of your values and priorities.

A discreet lifestyle

Cillian Murphy has deliberately chosen to lead a low-key lifestyle, away from the spotlight and the tabloids. He does not employ a personal stylist or agent, often traveling alone and attending events solo. His reserve and lack of interest in fame demonstrate his desire to protect his private life and concentrate on his work.

Murphy finds the red carpet experience stressful and avoids situations that might draw undue attention to himself. He prefers to live a simple and low-key life, which allows him to maintain a healthy balance between his career and personal life.

Murphy's low-key lifestyle is a conscious choice that reflects his values and priorities. He values authenticity, intimacy and time spent with loved ones. Avoiding the hype and excess associated with fame, Murphy creates a safe space for himself and his family, while pursuing his passion for performing.

Friendships and personal style

Cillian Murphy cultivates strong friendships, especially with other Irish actors like Colin Farrell, Jonathan Rhys Meyers and Liam Neeson. He considers Neeson a "surrogate father in cinema". However, his closest friendships are those he made before he became famous.

Murphy's personal style is understated and understated. In 2015, he was named one of GQ's 50 Best Dressed Men. Her fashion sense reflects her reserved character and aversion to excessive attention.

Murphy's friendships and personal style highlight the importance he places on authenticity and privacy. He values meaningful, lasting relationships, and he chooses clothing that reflects his identity and values rather than following trends or seeking public approval.

Authenticity and humility

Authenticity and humility are fundamental traits that define Cillian Murphy as an individual and as an artist.

He resisted the pressure to conform to celebrity expectations, choosing instead to live a simple, low-key life. Her close friendships, understated style of dress, and aversion to the spotlight demonstrate her commitment to authenticity.

Murphy's humility is reflected in his recognition of the role of luck and collaboration in his success. He has always expressed gratitude to those who have supported him throughout his career, and he remains approachable and down-to-earth despite his international fame.

Murphy's authenticity and humility are a breath of fresh air in the entertainment industry. They serve as a reminder that true value lies in character and achievements, rather than fame or wealth.

In his youth, Cillian Murphy adhered to an agnostic view, believing that it was impossible to know or prove the existence or non-existence of deities. This perspective allowed him to remain open to different spiritual beliefs without committing to a definitive position.

However, his involvement in the science fiction film " Sunshine " (2007) sparked a deep questioning of his religious beliefs. In this film, Murphy plays a nuclear physicist and astronaut on a perilous mission to reignite the dying sun.

The exploration of existential themes and confrontation with the fragility of life in " Sunshine " led Murphy to ask fundamental questions about the nature of the universe and the role of humanity. He began to doubt the presence of a benevolent divine being in the face of the suffering and tragedies plaguing the world.

After extensive introspection, Murphy decided to reject the idea of a creator God and embrace atheism. This belief, which denies the existence of all deities, brought him a feeling of clarification and intellectual freedom.

Murphy's spiritual journey from agnosticism to atheism is a testament to the profound influence that personal experiences and reflections can have on an individual's core beliefs.

Beyond his successful acting career, Cillian Murphy is also an ardent defender of social and political causes. Its commitment has been demonstrated through various initiatives, including:

Rock the Vote campaign (2007, Ireland): Murphy played an active role in this campaign to encourage young Irish voters to participate in the general election. He recognized the importance of civic engagement in shaping the future of the nation.

Homeless Rights Campaign with Focus Ireland: Murphy has partnered with Focus Ireland, an Irish charity dedicated to tackling homelessness. He has used his notoriety to raise awareness of this crucial issue and support efforts to provide housing and support to those in need.

Murphy's political involvement reflects his compassion and desire to contribute to a more just and equitable society. He recognizes the power of his voice and platform to amplify marginalized voices and advocate for necessary social changes.

His activism highlights the depth of his character, reaching beyond the spotlight to champion the causes he cares about.

In 2011, Cillian Murphy strengthened his social commitment by becoming a patron of the UNESCO Children and Families Research Center (UCFRC) at the National University of Ireland in Galway. This center is dedicated to research and promotion of the well-being of children and families.

Murphy made a close connection with the work of Professor Pat Dolan, Director of UCFRC and the UNESCO Chair on Children, Youth and Civic Engagement. Professor Dolan is a leading researcher in the field of youth civic engagement and has worked closely with Murphy on various initiatives aimed at empowering young people and giving them a voice in society.

Through his sponsorship of UCFRC, Murphy demonstrates his passion for supporting innovative research and programs that improve the lives of children and families. It recognizes the importance of creating a supportive environment where young people can thrive and contribute meaningfully to their communities.

Murphy's association with UCFRC highlights his commitment to using his platform to promote social causes and inspiring others to do the same. His support of research and youth-focused initiatives highlights his desire to create a better future for generations to come.

In February 2012, Cillian Murphy expressed solidarity with former workers at Vita Cortex, an Irish medical device factory, who were engaged in a sit-in to protest mass layoffs. In a message of support, Murphy praised their courage and determination to defend their rights.

Murphy's intervention in the case highlighted his commitment to supporting workers and fighting social injustices. He acknowledged the devastating impact of layoffs on workers and their families, and called for action to protect workers' rights.

Murphy's support for Vita Cortex is part of his broader activism for social and economic rights. He used his voice and platform to amplify the voices of the marginalized and advocate for positive change. His commitment to defending just causes demonstrates his compassion and his desire to contribute to a more equitable society.

Born on May 25, 1976 in Douglas, Ireland, Cillian Murphy is a renowned Irish actor and musician. His early musical aspirations led him to a career in rock, but his innate talent later drew him to theater. In the late 1990s, he started in short films and independent films.

Murphy's breakthrough came in 2002 with his captivating role in "28 Days Later." His performance in films such as "Return to Cold Mountain ", "Intermission", " Red Eye " and "Breakfast on Pluto " earned him a Golden Globe nomination in 2006.

He gained international fame playing Jonathan Crane, aka Scarecrow, in Christopher Nolan's acclaimed " Dark Knight" trilogy. His versatile talent was subsequently illustrated in "The Wind Rises", " Sunshine ", "The Edge of Love", " Inception " and "The Secret of Peacock ".

Continuing to shine both on the big screen and on stage, Cillian Murphy has established himself as a major player in the contemporary cinematic landscape.

In 2011, Cillian Murphy added new distinctions to his list of achievements: an Irish Times Theater Award for Best Actor and a Drama Desk Award for Outstanding Solo Performance in " Misterman ".

Beyond his artistic career, he became involved in social causes by becoming a patron of the UNESCO Center for Research on Children and Families at the National University of Ireland in Galway. He works closely with Professor Pat Dolan, Director of the Center and the UNESCO Chair on Children, Youth and Civic Engagement.

In the early 2010s, Murphy continued to shine on the big screen in films such as "In Time," " Retreat " and " Red Lights." His versatile talent and commitment to challenging roles have cemented his position among the most respected actors of his generation.

From 2013 to 2022, Cillian Murphy played the charismatic Thomas "Tommy" Shelby, the lead in the hit series " Peaky Blinders ". His masterful performance earned him two Irish

Film and Television Awards for Best Actor – Drama, in 2017 and 2018.

Alongside his iconic role in " Peaky Blinders ", Murphy continued to explore various characters in cinema. He notably starred in "Transcendence", "In the Heart of the Ocean", "Operation Anthropoid ", "Dunkirk", "The Delinquent Season ", "Anna" and "Quietly 2".

His ability to portray complex characters and bring compelling stories to life has cemented his reputation as an exceptional, versatile and talented actor.

In 2023, Cillian Murphy reached new heights in his career with his stunning portrayal of J. Robert Oppenheimer in the acclaimed Christopher Nolan biopic, "Oppenheimer." His masterful performance won him the Golden Globe for Best Actor in a Motion Picture Drama, the British Academy Film Award for Best Actor and the Academy Award for Best Actor.

This prestigious recognition is a testament to Murphy's exceptional talent and ability to portray complex and captivating characters.

In 2020, the Irish Times ranked him 12th of the best Irish actors, highlighting his undeniable contribution to Irish and international cinema.

Cillian Murphy 's career continues to be marked by unforgettable performances and well-deserved awards, cementing his status as a leading actor in the global cinematic landscape.

Born in the picturesque town of Douglas, Ireland, Cillian Murphy grew up in the studious atmosphere of Ballintemple. His father, Brendan, was a civil servant in the Irish Department of Education, while his mother passed on her passion for the French language as a teacher. The family heritage of teaching also extended to his grandparents, aunts and uncles.

From a young age, Murphy developed a strong interest in music and writing, composing songs from the age of 10. He also has a younger brother, Páidi, and two younger sisters, Sile and Orla. This close-knit brotherhood helped shape his childhood and fuel his creative imagination.

In this intellectually and artistically stimulating home environment, Murphy's innate talents began to blossom, laying the foundation for his successful career in show business.

As a youth, Cillian Murphy was raised Catholic and attended Presentation Brothers College, a Catholic secondary school. Although academically brilliant, he was also known for his turbulent spirit until his fourth year.

Sports played a major role in school life to the detriment of creative pursuits, a regret Murphy later expressed. It was at high school that he discovered his passion for the stage thanks to a theater module led by Pat Kiernan, director of Corcadorca Theater Company. It was a revelation for Murphy, who later described the feeling of feeling "fully alive" on stage.

His English teacher, the poet and novelist William Wall, was instrumental in his journey by encouraging him to pursue a career in acting. This idea resonated with Murphy, who also aspired to become a rock star, seeing both vocations as a way to express his creativity and connect with audiences.

When he was around 20, Cillian Murphy embraced his passion for music, forming several bands with his brother Páidi. They drew inspiration from the catchy melodies of the Beatles and the eccentric musical experiments of Frank Zappa, known for his "wacky lyrics and endless guitar solos."

Despite the enticing offer of a five-album deal, Murphy and his band ultimately chose to decline. This decision was a testament to their determination to maintain their artistic integrity and continue their musical journey on their own terms.

After declining the record deal, Cillian Murphy continued his quest for creative expression. He found a new home for his talent on the theater stage, where he could explore complex characters and tell compelling stories.

His notable stage performances attracted the attention of directors, and Murphy soon made his screen debut in short films and independent productions. His raw talent and undeniable charisma allowed him to land bigger roles, including in critically acclaimed films such as "28 Days Later" and "Return to Cold Mountain."

Over the years, Murphy has cemented his reputation as a versatile and captivating actor, capable of portraying a wide range of characters, from stoic heroes to tortured villains. His masterful portrayal of Jonathan Crane, aka the Scarecrow, in Christopher Nolan's " Dark Knight" trilogy was particularly memorable, earning him praise from critics and audiences alike.

Alongside his thriving film career, Murphy has remained true to his theatrical roots, regularly appearing on stage in critically acclaimed productions. His unwavering commitment to the craft of acting and his ability to bring unforgettable characters to life have made him one of the most respected and in-demand stars in show business.

While a promising law student at the University of Cork (UCC) in 1996, Cillian Murphy realized his heart was not in that path. Despite his academic abilities, he failed his exams, admitting that he had no ambition to pursue law.

His passion for music and theater was too strong to ignore. He chose to devote his time and energy to his musical career, forming several bands with his brother and performing regularly on stage. The lure of creative expression and the ability to tell compelling stories ultimately outweighed his interest in law.

By dropping out of law school, Murphy followed his true calling and paved the way for his successful acting career.

A captivating performance of A Clockwork Orange, directed by his theatrical mentor Pat Kiernan, reignited Cillian Murphy's interest in acting. He landed his first major role in Observe the Sons of Ulster Marching Towards the Somme, a poignant play which explored the horrors of the First World War.

Murphy also had the lead role in Little Shop of Horrors, a quirky musical comedy performed at the Cork Opera House. Although he admitted that his initial motivations were more focused on social interactions than a true aspiration for an acting career, this experience sowed the seeds of his passion for the stage.

Over time, Murphy realized that his true calling was to bring characters to life and tell stories through the power of acting. His natural talent and unwavering dedication paved the way for his successful career on stage and screen.

As Cillian Murphy continued to explore the world of acting, he realized that his true passion lay in the ability to transform into different characters and tell stories through acting. His natural talent and unwavering dedication paved the way for his successful career on stage and screen.

He landed his first television role in "The Way We Live Now ", a six-part adaptation of the eponymous novel by Anthony Trollope. His remarkable performance attracted the attention of movie directors, and soon Murphy made his big screen debut in the drama "Disco Pigs ", at the sides of Elaine Cassidy.

Murphy's breakthrough role came in 2002 when he played the lead in "28 Days Later," a post-apocalyptic horror film that became a cult classic. His portrayal of a determined and vulnerable survivor earned him praise from critics and audiences.

Since then, Murphy has starred in a wide range of critically acclaimed films, including "Return to Cold Mountain ", "Batman Begins ", " Inception " and "Dunkirk". He also continued to appear on stage, in productions such as " Misterman " and "The Lieutenant of Inishmore ".

With his versatile talent, undeniable charisma and commitment to the craft of acting, Cillian Murphy has become one of the most respected and in-demand stars in show business.

In 1995, determined to pursue his passion for theater, Cillian Murphy approached Pat Kiernan, the artistic director of the Corcadorca Theater Company, and persuaded him to let him audition. Despite initial hesitation, Kiernan eventually gave in to Murphy's repeated urgings.

During his audition, Murphy demonstrated raw talent and undeniable stage presence. Kiernan was impressed by his passion and dedication, and offered him a role in the company's production of "A Clockwork Orange".

This opportunity marked a turning point in Murphy's career. Her captivating performance in "A Clockwork Orange" caught the attention of critics and audiences, and paved the way for larger roles in theater and film.

Murphy's journey is a testament to his unwavering perseverance and belief in his dream of becoming an actor. His talent, coupled with his tenacity, allowed him to overcome obstacles and realize his ambitions on stage and screen.

Throughout his distinguished career, Cillian Murphy has received numerous prestigious accolades for his outstanding on-screen performances. His awards are a testament to his talent, dedication and the global recognition he has received for his work.

- Best Actor, Ourense Independent Film Festival 2002 for his role in "Disco Pigs "

- Best Actor, Irish Film and Television Awards 2007 - for his role in "Breakfast on Pluto "

- Best Cast, Circuit Community Awards 2008 Awards for his role in "The Dark Knight", shared with an exceptional cast

- Best actor in a dramatic television series, Festival international des programs audiovisuels de Biarritz 2014 for his role in " Peaky Blinders "

- Best Actor in a Television Drama Series, Irish Film and Television Awards 2017, 2018 for his role in " Peaky Blinders "

- Best Actor in a Drama Television Series, TV Choice Awards 2018 for his role in " Peaky Blinders "

- Best Actor in a Television Series Drama, National Television Awards 2020 - for his role in " Peaky Blinders "

- Best Supporting Actor, Hollywood Critics Association Midseason Awards 2021 – for his role in "Without a sound 2"

- Best actor, BAFTA 2024 - for his role in "Oppenheimer"

- Best actor in a drama film, Golden Globes 2024 - for his role in "Oppenheimer"

- Best Actor, Oscars 2024 – for his role in "Oppenheimer"

- Best Actor, Screen Actors Guild Awards 2024 - for his role in "Oppenheimer"

Murphy's awards are a testament to his artistic depth and ability to portray complex and emotional characters. His performances captivated audiences and earned him the respect of his peers in the film industry.

In addition to his numerous awards, Cillian Murphy has also received numerous nominations for his outstanding on-screen performances. These nominations recognize his talent and ability to bring complex and memorable characters to life:

- Most Promising Actor, Empire Awards 2003 - for her role in "28 Days Later"

- Best Actor and Most Promising Actor, Irish Film and Television Awards 2003 - for his roles in "Disco Pigs " and "28 Days Later"

- Best Actor, Fangoria Chainsaw Awards 2004 - for his role in "28 Days Later"

- Best actor and best revelation across the Atlantic, MTV Movie Awards 2004 - for his role in "28 Days Later"

- Best Actor, Online Film Critics Society Awards 2004 - for his role in "28 Days Later"

- Best Actor, Irish Film and Television Awards 2005 - for his role in " Red Eye : Under high pressure"

- Best Supporting Actor, Irish Film and Television Awards 2005 - for his role in "Batman Begins "

- Best Actor, Satellite Awards 2005 – for his role in "Breakfast on Pluto "

- Best Actor, St. Louis Film Critics Association Awards 2005 - for his role in "The Wind Rises"

Murphy's nominations reflect the recognition of his talent by his peers in the film industry. His ability to portray a wide range of characters with depth and nuance has made him one of the most in-demand and respected actors of his generation.

The year 2006 was particularly successful for Cillian Murphy, who received numerous nominations and awards for his exceptional performances:

- Best Actor, Iris h Independent Film Awards 2006 - for his role in "The Wind Rises"

- Best Actor, Dublin Film Critics Circle Awards 2006 - for his role in "The Wind Rises"

- Best Actor, European Film Prize 2006 - for his roles in "Breakfast on Pluto " and "Le vent se leva" (jointly awarded)

- British Actor of the Year in a Supporting Role, London Critics Circle Film Awards 2006 - for his role in "Batman Begins "

- Best Villain, MTV Movie Awards 2006 - for his role in "Batman Begins "

- Best Actor, Golden Globes 2006 - for his role in "Breakfast on Pluto " (nomination)

- Best Supporting Actor, Saturn Awards 2006- for his role in " Red Eye : Under high pressure"

- Best scoundrel, Teen Choice Awards 2006 - for his roles in "Batman Begins " and " Red Eye : Under high pressure"

These nominations and awards highlight the worldwide recognition of Murphy's talent and his ability to portray complex and memorable characters. His portrayal of diverse characters, from romantic heroes to charismatic villains, has captivated audiences and earned him the admiration of his peers in the film industry.

The years 2007 to 2011 were marked by further accolades for Cillian Murphy, including:

- Rising Star Award, British Academy Film Awards 2007 – for his role in " Sunshine "

- Best Actor, Irish Film and Television Awards 2008 - for his role in " Sunshine "

- Davis Award for Best Cast, Awards Circuit Community Awards 2010 - for his role in " Inception ", shared with an exceptional cast

- Best Cast, Scream Awards 2010 - for his role in " Inception "

- Best Cast, Phoenix Film Critics Society Awards 2010 - for her role in " Inception "

- Best Cast, Washington DC Area Film Critics Association Awards 2010 - for role in " Inception "

- Best Cast, Central Ohio Film Critics Association Awards 2011 – for role in " Inception "

- Best Cast, Gold Derby Awards 2011 - for her role in " Inception "

- Best Supporting Actor, Irish Film and Television Awards 2011- for his role in " Inception "

- Best Actor in a Leading Role, Irish Film and Television Awards 2011 - for his role in " Perrier's Bounty"

These awards recognize Murphy's outstanding contribution to outstanding ensembles, as well as his ability to portray complex and memorable characters in both lead and supporting roles. Her performance in " Inception," in particular, was praised by critics for its emotional depth and magnetic screen presence.

Cillian Murphy 's accolades continued through the 2010s and beyond:

- Best Cast, International Online Cinema Awards 2011 - for his role in " Inception "

- Best Cast, Online Film & Television Association Awards 2011 - for her role in " Inception "

- Best Supporting Actor, British Independent Film Awards 2012 – for his role in " Broken "

- Best Actor in a Television Drama Series, Irish Film and Television Awards 2015 - for his role in " Peaky Blinders "

- Best Actor, Czech Lions 2017 - for his role in "Operation Anthropoid "

- Most Popular Actor in a TV Drama Series, National Television Awards 2017 - for his role in " Peaky Blinders "

- Best Drama Actor in a Television Drama Series, National Television Awards 2019 - for his role in " Peaky Blinders "

- Saturn Award for Best Actor in a Motion Picture, Saturn Awards 2024 - for his role in "Oppenheimer".

These awards highlight Murphy's versatility as an actor, his ability to bring complex and memorable characters to life in films and television series. His portrayal of Thomas Shelby in " Peaky Blinders " brought him worldwide recognition and immense success with audiences and critics.

In conclusion, Cillian Murphy is a critically acclaimed Irish actor whose versatility and exceptional talent have earned him worldwide fame. From his breakthrough role in "28 Days Later" to his haunting portrayal of Tommy Shelby in " Peaky Blinders," Murphy left an indelible mark on film and television.

His intensity, his charismatic presence and his ability to embody complex and tormented characters have made him an actor very appreciated by the public and the film industry. As his career continues to grow, there is no doubt that Cillian Murphy will continue to captivate and inspire audiences for many years to come.

Printed in Great Britain
by Amazon